THESE POEMS ARE ABOUT SUNNY DAYS

by Nikki Van Ekeren

Imprint: Independently published

For information regarding permission or distribution, contact **nikkivanekeren@gmail.com**

To discover more about the author visit
nikkivanekeren.com

ISBN: 978-0-578-63511-8

creating a sunny day
is a collaboration,
a partnership
between
you and life.

chapter 1
the sacred expression

chapter 2
the palm tree

chapter 7
exploring the terrain

chapter one

the sacred expression

01

the sacred expression

witnessing the divine
move through my body,
my heart
and my mind
is an honor.
this flow occurs within
each one of us
whether we are aware of it or not.
it is the way we receive
love from our source.
it is unconditionally generous
with every human being.
it is pure unbridled joy.

this gift is also the
most challenging expression
to receive,
to interpret,
to share,
and to feel worthy of.
this gift can be the cause
of severe discomfort in the body
when we do not know how to accommodate it.

we may feel unequipped
and unworthy
to accept such glory.
it is almost as if our little bodies
reject such divine offerings at first.

once we can understand
that the sacred longs
to express itself
through us,
we can surrender and allow it in.
we can learn how to
open up to
the purest form of love
and watch it transform us.
we can witness this sacred expression
from within and around
and be present in all its magic.
we can stop resisting
and truly experience
and be in
the flow
of this beautiful life.

02

reaching for life

i accept my strength.
i act with this inner awareness.
i move with the flow of life,
jumping into ideal opportunities.
i am here to grow,
to stretch,
to expand,
to feel my power.

i accept the good
that wants to greet me.
i greet the humans
that want to help me.
i love the community
that wants to support me.

life welcomes me
when i reach for it.

03

deciding not to hear the noise

making the decision to exist
above the chatter
of what others think
changes everything.

the inner tension
disappears.
creations emerge
from spaces within
that you did not know were there.
worries cease.
you begin to glow again.

the noise will always
want to steer your course.
acknowledge its presence.
charge ahead.
you can do this.

04

feeling comfortable in your power

you have a
power deep within you
that you've been taught to suppress,
to hide,
to silence.
when we can
accept this,
we can free our power.
we can begin
to feel comfortable using
this tool
this power
to navigate the world.

this immediately changes
our lens from
victim
to creator.
we can see
our gifts and talents more clearly
and share them with the world.
we can vocalize our needs and wants.

we can work hard,
be present,
and feel successful.

say the words
"i feel comfortable in my power."
allow this to be your
inner mantra.

05

i forge ahead

i walk straight ahead
into the pain,
into the resistance.
i feel the discomfort this triggers,
yet i proceed with my
head held high.

i get to do this.
i get to persist
until i succeed.
i get to allow joy
into my life.
i get to unblock
the clogged passageways within.

after all,
this is all truly a gift.
one that i've created
especially for me.

06

the gift of today

rest into today,
life is a miracle.

life is so big.
don't limit yourself
to what's comfortable.

can you recognize
the gift of this day?
the dark night
allowed the stars
to shine through
while you slumbered.
you arose to hear birds singing
and the sun's rays
hugging your soul.
you are here.
you get to be you.

allow this miracle to seep in.
this is life.
let it create you.

07

staying true to me

you should be doing this,
your focus should be here,
you could've made more money this way...
and the list goes on.
there will always be someone
telling you how
you should be living your life.
the key in this equation
is who you listen to.
you
are the only one
who knows what's best for you.

are you blossoming
and emerging
and discovering
who you are
in an organic way?
then don't rush it.
you don't need more
money,
accolades,
or followers
to prove to yourself who you are.

those that do not look ahead
to the long term
forget that this journey
continues.
there's no end
with the accomplishment of a goal.

the need for inner peace,
self love
and self confidence
is universal.
as we can observe with
those that have come before us,
it's the inner discussions
we have with ourselves
that are the most important habits.

good habits will
always find success.
there truly is no rush.
honor your body's timeline.
a thriving spirit
may not need
the attention of the masses to soar.

08

words can heal

empowering words
sharpen our mental capacity
and our ability to grow.
healing words
mixed with a wholesome intention
create long lasting change.
words are the bridge
to empowerment.
we can change
when we put in the work.

often, too many of us
suffer because of false superstitions
that have been passed down
for hundreds of years.

rational thinking
cuts through these lies.
irrational thinking
creates suffering.

when we can pull ourselves
out of irrational thoughts, superstitions,
and projected problems,

we can see ourselves more clearly.
there is always potential
in the moment.

happiness is attainable
when you're willing to do the work.
let go of the habitual
thought patterns.
accept the reality you're in
and move on.
one can learn how to think logically
if they surrender
their projected identity.

people see you as you are
not as you pretend to be.
let go of blaming.
let go of shaming
yourself and others.
if you'd have known better,
you'd have done better.
start doing better now
with empowering words
at the core.

09

roots

as i begin to learn more about
my roots
and lineage,
i can see more clearly
into the patterns that i embody.
why have we passed down
the pain,
the hurt,
the anger,
the shame,
the jealousy?
why do we teach one another
how to cope with life
by reliving its darkest moments?
i honor those
who came before me,
but i honor my soul's mission more.
as i face the discomfort within,
the habits seem to lose their power
over me.
they surface from inside of me,
so they are a part of my story.

as with any emotion,

.

its life begins inside of the body
and then manifests itself in our
external world.
we can stop this cycle
when we recognize it.
the painful emotions
that emerge from the depths of our being
can be extinguished as quickly
as their creation.
the silent pause
before you proclaim the inner emotion
is the key moment.

with every sensory organ,
to see,
to touch,
to taste,
to hear,
to smell...
we separate our sensation
with its ownership.
how do we transfer this quality to
our inner emotional world?
you can feel something,

yet, you do not own it.

begin with this moment.

what are you feeling?

it is not you.

it is a feeling inside of you.

let it go.

the roots of our emotions

run so deep

that to dig them up by their origins

is a lifelong task.

choose to observe them.

choose to honor your roots.

they are here

to sculpt your being.

10

there's no turning back now

the growing pains
that accompany becoming
my best self
no longer frighten me.
they entice me
to surrender to this life.

the intelligence within me
is steering my psyche
and will show me
where to go.
i am aware
yet obedient
to the calls.

there is no need to look backward
only forward.
love is guiding me
and i feel its embrace
at every turn.

11

the life force

i am propelled
by the life force
inside of me.
its intelligence
far surpasses mine.
it guides me
into the depths
of joy.

at first it may appear
that this force
is steering me into fear,
but those feelings of uncertainty
open up passageways
into nirvana.

the life force
inside of me
is inside of you
and all living things.
it is in charge
and we are its humble observers.
when we realize
that we are not in control,

we can rest into life.

life,
i answer to your call.
show me the wonders
of this journey.

12

life, i love you

oh life,
i love you.
you greet me
where i am at
and challenge me
to go further.

oh life,
i love you.
you slow me down
and grab my attention
when i get steered
off my intended course.

oh life,
i love you.
you inspire me
to accept myself
and see myself
as our perfect little creation.

oh life,
i love you.
you comfort me
when i feel fearful
and assure me
that there is nothing to worry about.

oh life,
i love you.
thank you for
this partnership.
you treat me with kindness
and teach me how to
treat myself and others the same.

oh life,
i love you.

van ekeren

chapter two

the palm tree

01

take a moment

you've been working on the inner
for quite some time.
it has taken you this long
to get exactly where you are at.
appreciate how far you've come.
revel in your experiences.

rest in your energy
and feel its authenticity.
you have worked hard to get here.

allow the future to excite you.
there are endless possibilities
when you believe in yourself.

02

nature is

she is powerful.
she is confident.
she is passionate.
she does not waiver.
she can create.
she can destroy.

she is nature.

she can gently nourish
a small and silent seed,
yet has the ability to destroy miles of
mature and fertile land.
she opens up to anyone willing to listen,
but does not overcompensate
for the ignorant.

she is teaching us through metaphors
every moment of every day.
the question is,
do we have the eyes to see her magic?

03

the palm tree

your silhouette
evokes a sense
of luxury and ecstasy.

when one sees your likeness,
they give themselves
permission
to enjoy.

you have carefully curated
the surroundings in which you thrive,
basking only in exotic and warm locales.

you share your wisdom
with your admirers
and encourage them
to seek quality of life
over any other thing.

your quiet power
is met with an understated grace.
you have inspired us all
with your ease.

when i sit under a palm tree,
i feel your bohemian vibe.

oh palm tree,
thanks for sharing your wonder.

04

to accept

i generously give my mind
the space to accept
my life
exactly as it is.
i have worked hard to get here.
i have created the woman that i am.

i choose to accept where i am at.
i choose to act with kindness in my heart
and gumption in my belly.

this decision builds a bridge
from my mind to my heart
that cannot be broken by outside influences.
i get to choose
the future
by the lens in which i view it.

i accept my life
my choices
my outcomes.

from a bird's eye view,
everything will always appear perfect.

this distance makes room
for wisdom.
from the lens of the flesh,
things may appear stressful and more
important than they actually are.
seeing through the lens of self identity
can bend and morph things
out of focus.

i reach to my highest point of view
to see the continual flow
of beauty
in my life.
after all,
it is only beauty and love in the end.

05

to forgive

i forgive myself.
i forgive those that taught me
their fearful ways.
i forgive those that hurt me.

i forgive my mind for repeating
my missteps to me,
for you are only trying to protect me.
i understand how to talk myself through this
and transmute this energy into confidence.

i forgive my heart
for closing off at times.
i choose to continue to work on opening it.

i forgive my body.
i only send you love.

i forgive my human nature.
i am here,
i am human.
i will continue to make mistakes.
i will persist in the journey to forgive myself.

06

to ask

ask for what you truly want
in life.
if you want to heal;
ask to heal.
if you want to be seen;
ask to be seen.
if you want to thrive;
ask to thrive.
it is this simple.
the art of asking
with an open heart
will produce magical results.
ask for what you want.
do not circle around your desire
to appear above asking.

to seek
is to know
and embody humility.
this experience
satiates the soul.

07

one plus one

there is a certain magic
that is created
when two people share
their truths with one another.
this bonding experience
releases the divine
as if it were the
seeds of a dandelion
being blown
on a windy day.
to exhibit this courage
and become vulnerable
in front of another
is love,
is true love.

to open up with grace
to another seems to
alert the invisible realms
of your bravery.
the unseen guides
heed the call
and help you grow.
your discomfort or pain

is transmuted into strength
and clarity.
you begin to understand why
you had to dig deep
and experience this transformation.

it came so innocently from the heart,
yet this willingness to share
has opened up caverns within.
you feel anew,
refreshed
and able to fully trust.
the one who you shared with
feels this too.
your bond has grown
and will never go backward.

this new level
of loving
and living
will forever continue
when you share from your heart
with grace.

08

always trying

if you are continually
trying your hardest,
then why worry
about the end result.

in the now,
you are trying.
you are giving life your best effort.
be in your skin,
and your mind,
and know
that this is enough.

these poems are about sunny days

van ekeren

these poems are about sunny days

chapter three

nature is my muse

01

nature is my muse

nature
is
my
muse.

she boldly shows me
how to grow,
how to be,
how to see.

nature does not worry
what the world will think of her,
she expresses herself
with no regrets.

the storm erupts with no announcement,
the temperature of the air touches
all around it,
the rain pours on those who ask for it and
those who don't,
the trees continue to grow and take up space.

nature is my ultimate muse.
i hope to be as strong
as she is.
i hope to be as free
to be me
as she is,
never pandering
or wondering what others will think.

02

the art of possibility

i used to visualize an external success
and then work toward it,
to feel the rewarding feeling of
future happiness.
my goals emerged from this way of thinking.
i would ask myself,
"what does my external world need
so i can feel happy on the inside?"

as i was walking home this morning,
i felt so happy
and joyful
and content.
i had just merely walked to
my usual coffee shop
and then sipped my coffee
on my journey home.
there was no epic change
or goal that was met.
something shifted
and awakened on the inside.
i felt happy
in the moment
and knew this was something i could

always tap into.

there is no scarcity of joy
in our world.
there are just different views of
how we see.

when we see possibility,
we feel good.
when we see scarcity,
we don't feel good.

what if
we could begin to
not be swayed by external temptations
and grow deep roots
into our soul's soil?
the possibilities of how to be happy
are endless.
it is available to us all
inside of our own bodies.

03

just because it is offered

just because one asks something of me
doesn't mean that i must accept.

why do i feel so weary
when asked?
why do i cringe when i
want to say no?
origins of habits run deep.
my reasons may not
reveal themselves to me.
can i accept that?

the soil does not blame its caretakers
when it lacks,
nor does the tree complain
when it needs water.
the wounded animal does not
seek its predator for revenge,
rather it focuses its energy on healing.

when certain traits emerge
from within my psyche
that i do not particularly enjoy,
i shall accept them

and not project blame.
i shall not focus my strength
on feelings of victimhood or blame.
i will begin to move forward
and see how this is part of healing.

how does this relate to being asked
and then saying no?

i am learning how to break a habit
and not exude guilt onto myself.
i am working on myself.
i am letting old triggers dissolve.

04

the great gesture

you get to be here.
you get to be you.
why not enjoy every part of this ride?

even in the midst of
a hard chapter,
this is the only book
you continually create.
the doubt,
the fear,
the pain
are traits
of being human.
you can change how
you handle them.
are you truly in pain?
or are you painfully against
your reality?
accepting life
as it is
right now
is freeing.

this is the great gesture.
once you accept reality,
you cannot have anxiety.
the two cannot coexist.
acceptance enables flow.
acceptance makes change easy.
acceptance allows inner stillness.
acceptance does not
mean complacency.
it means a willingness to forge ahead
no matter what.
acceptance ignites rational thinking
and lessens fears.

sure, your life may not be
exactly how you'd choose,
but it is happening.
so, why go to battle?
acceptance brings honor
and responsibility.
ask for help
from above
to live in a constant
state of acceptance.

05

to repeat your message

when you begin to
clearly define
and repeat your message,
the needed courage emerges.
you begin to resonate
the energy of your objective
and live by it.
your actions and words
reinforce your intention.

to understand the art of repetition
one needs to see the significance
in the cadence it offers.
the human brain needs repetition to learn.
your message will not be heard
unless you repeat yourself.

the untrained psyche
shies away from repetition
for fear of rejection,
while the educated psyche
revels in this art.
sharing your message
with clarity and ease

allows one to succeed in their work
and find the right audience.
your words match your purpose.
you seek right action through repetition
rather than validation through conformity.

06

unraveling a thread

every feeling has a beginning
when it surfaces within your body.
where and how did it originate?
who taught you to feel this way?
unravel the mystery
by asking the questions.
the answers will gently flow to you
bringing your truth.

you will understand your human nature
and honor your journey.
you will nurture your wounds
allowing them to heal properly.
you will feel no more shame
because the act of being human
is a brave journey.
your emotions and feelings are a byproduct
of your entire existence.
to remove one
would change your entire demeanor.

it is not about getting rid of feelings,
it is learning how to get through them.
there is no blame to bestow

when you know
that everyone in your life
is doing their best.
your goal is to grow exponentially,
to experience emotions without identifying
with them,
to honor your spirit and never feel blame,
to show compassion to yourself and others
and to radiate pure love.

getting in touch with your emotions
is the bridge
from the body to the spirit.

07

i love how metaphors crawl out of nature

when i do not feel aligned
and the ways of the world
have tugged at my heart,
i often take a walk in nature.
she cheers me right up,
reminding me that
those tugs are actually making me stronger.

the metaphors of self acceptance
crawl out of every beautiful living thing.
i walk by the birds
who have landed on the ground
and joyfully hop along.
they're not envious of me and
my ability to walk better.
i walk by the old trees
with exposed roots coiling
up through the grass.
they're not apologizing for taking up space.
i walk by the pond
whose water appears as still as glass.
she allows all visitors into her splendor
with no fear of their back story.

my walks in nature
have helped me calm down
and allowed me
to see who I am at my core.
what am i rushing around for?
who am i trying to be?
i have always been right here.
thanks nature
for your wisdom
and inclusive ability
to help us see ourselves in you.

08

sink into the rhythm of love

the natural rhythm of life is love.

the motion of breathing,
the waves of the ocean,
the movement of clouds in the sky
evoke a certain momentum.
it is purposeful,
yet poetic.
this rhythm never ceases
nor discriminates.
its simplicity illuminates.
its powerful energy
demands contemplation.

when we can sink into this rhythm,
we thrive and radiate with possibilities.
we exude our unique life force.
we do not get stuck in drama
because there's no need for it.
our attention is fully focused
on our intention, on our power.
the natural rhythm of life
passionately releases love
that sings.

09

as the truth spills out

i used to hide my eyes and ears
from the truth.
i did not know that
when the truth reveals itself,
there's no judgement.

the truth has no sharp edges,
for it is like water
that rushes over everything it touches.
the terrain of one's psyche
will be forever changed
when the truth floods its walls.

the truth has no desire
to make anyone happy
or enable one's uneducated decisions.
it exists to inform.
it penetrates when one is ready to hear it.

when the truth is experienced,
it strengthens all who listen.
one may wait decades to have
the ability to receive their truth.
take no judgement in this.

the soil of your mind
needed to be tended to.

once you've heard the truth,
let it soak in.
share it.
bask in it.
it is your gift.
you do not need to hide any longer.

these poems are about sunny days

van ekeren

chapter four

the beach

01

the beach

you reach

my soul

and show me

my potential.

you see me.

you breathe

through me.

you inspire

me

to see

me.

my potential.

my worth.

my abilities.

my stability.

my nobility.

there is no need

to fear

my greatness

for i see

myself

as the sea.

02

be that person

you know those people
that everything just works out for?

what is it about them?
it is their perspective.
it is how they view their life.
they are sharing their version
of life with you
and all they see is the good stuff.

sure, not everything works out according
to plan,
but they smile through it all.
it is not their circumstances,
but their outlook
that flavors their life.

this way of living
is open to everyone.
it is a moment by moment choice.

so,
be that person
that everything just works out for.

van ekeren

03

to climb that mountain

the earth's ability to
create mountains from land
still astounds me.
these mystical
natural structures
ooze metaphorical stories
by their very presence.
how many internal mountains
have we learned to climb?

the physical act of hiking or climbing
gives its participant a visual goal
in the horizon;
to get to the top of the mountain.
how one approaches the summit
is their own personal journey.

the middle ground
may offer challenges and stumbling blocks
that can throw the journeyer off balance.
getting back up
and feeling that inner resilience
sends a sense of achievement through
the body.

one foot in front of the other,
one step at a time
and eventually
one will get to the top
of their mountain.

04

when i feel like myself

when i do not allow
what others think,
how others feel,
or another's judgements about me
fog my perception,
i feel like myself.

when i do not hunger for quick results
and allow nature to nurture
on its own time,
i feel like myself.

when i understand that
all good things take time
and bask in the present moment,
i feel like myself.

when i part ways with
humans who do not make me feel happy,
i feel like myself.

when i continue creating
what is in my heart
and in my soul

regardless of what the market
values worthy,
i feel like myself.

when i stay true to my values
and face the opposing forces with
assertiveness,
i feel like myself.

when i am the hero of my story,
i feel like myself.

05

to remember

i remember yesterday
with no regret.
i will remember today
with no judgement.
for i am a little human
trying my best.

i do not proclaim to know anything,
yet i strive to find answers continually.
i exist at this time
as this person
for a reason.
no matter how grandiose or small
it may be.
my truth matters.
my past matters.
my presence matters.

when i recall my past,
i can replay it all
with no guilt or shame.
this is the gift i give to myself.
i work to continue this way of living
knowing it is my birthright.

06

walking on air

as i went on my morning walk,
my mind was searching for memories
to land on.
this one
or that one.

which one to focus on?

i gave my mind
a little help.
today can be anything i want
it to be.
let's think about
a memory that brings
a smile to my face.

so, i did just that.

07

wash away the past

just like the waves
continually wash onto the shore,
time will continue
to tick on.
we are taught to
fear the results of time.
yet, it has magical healing powers.

it has the ability
to wash away the past
and take the sting out of
intense memories,
when we allow it.
time has the power
to wash away pain.

do not fear the results of time.
embrace its offerings.
wisdom is acquired and intensified over time,
just as gratitude and true love are.
nature knows far more than we do
and allows her creatures to
thrive in the wake of time.

08

the freedom

when you accept
the world
as it is
and not how you think it should be,
an internal freedom arises.
when you accept
your place in the world
as it is and not what you think it should be,
this same feeling of freedom
shifts your lens
and you begin to see
yourself in new ways.

you see your rare beauty
that you've always had.
you see your worth
regardless of what the world sees.
you take responsibility
for the path you've taken
and the one you will embark upon.

when you accept
who you are and where you came from,
an internal alchemical change takes place.

you accept your roots,

your lineage,

your story

with honor and grace.

you do not judge yourself

or those like you

as harshly.

you take pride in your feelings.

accepting your truth and beauty

fosters more acceptance

which opens the door to receiving abundance.

you allow the goodness to enter your world.

you do not fight harmony

for you now know

that you are the harmonious creature

that you've always aspired to become.

09

i choose joy

as life presents new challenges to me,
my physical body
wants to run away
from this discomfort.
my ego works extensively
to make sure that I am safe
from such disruptions.
I hear suggestions
from within such as
"take the easier way"
or "don't overextend yourself"
or even "poor you."

at first,
i rest into these emotions.
after all,
i want to be safe.
life can be so scary at times.

it's at this moment
when i have a choice.
do i sit with self made excuses
and justifications
and enable my fear to control me

or do i choose joy
and walk through the pain and discomfort?

i choose joy.
and then i choose joy
again and again.

sometimes i have no idea
why i'm smiling,
but i still smile.
i understand that life
takes place in my daily decisions.
there's so much out there to explore.
i choose to jump into life
willingly and openly
rather than hide from its glory.

this choice does not
take away the fear or pain,
but it helps me recognize it
as fuel.
this choice is not a one time deal.
i am working to make it a habit
and know that i'm not

going through this alone.
i will be constantly guided and led
on my journey.

my team of invisible· forces
has taken my cue.
joy is the gold
in this treasure map.

slowly,
my eyes and ears will adapt
and be on the constant lookout
for life's tender slices of joy.
those small moments
that exude wonder and awe
that i may have overlooked in prior times.
i rest into this lifestyle
with a calm
yet zesty demeanor.

woah,
things just got really fun.

van ekeren

chapter five

a tree never hides

01

a tree never hides

a tree never stunts its
growth for those
around it.
why should you?

our growth
is like that of the roots of
trees growing
underground.
we don't see the tangled mess
of the root system,
rather we see the finished
product - a healthy tree.

just by being you,
odds are that you will
eventually
offend someone,
hurt someone,
challenge someone
or make someone feel
uncomfortable.
when you claim your space,
just as when those trees

claim their turf for their roots,
you're taking a stand.

take up space.
grow those roots
and watch how
everything will organically
take shape.

our energetic space
is just as important as the roots
of a tree.
it's our foundation.
it's where we take
our mind's eye when we need
to reconnect.

02

our earth suit

we bravely agree
to journey to earth
in this human suit
to connect more deeply to our essence.
the soul that we inhabit
has to work harder to reach us
through the density of the earth's field
and our body's sensory system.
we suffer.
we fight.
we cry.
we surrender.
then, we soar.
there's no easy way
to journey inside
for the road is windy
and there is no map.

the invisible forces at work
within and around us
guide us
while we try to grasp what is occurring.
the love that we generate
continues to grow

during this process.
it may not appear as gracefully
as we'd prefer
and we will hurt others.
when a tree grows roots
it must take ownership of its space
or it will die,
just as we must exclaim who we are
or we will perish.
we must not be frightened of our power
and allow others to see our strength.

exude force,
speak with clarity,
make waves
all while constantly reconnecting
directly to that inner voice.
allow the earth suit
to do its job
and not encumber your evolution.
the journey is meant to work
through work.
the journey is our gift
to our self.

03

gritty and pretty

to feel gritty and pretty
at the same time
and not apologize for your strength.

to be free enough
to express your passion
and stand by your creations.

to feel your beauty
regardless of what you're wearing or
who sees you.

to know that social media is
neither bad nor good.
it is how one uses it
in their life.

to have the courage to
be seen
and heard
on a good or bad day.

to know that all things pass
and every new triumph or loss
will add to the layering of a life well lived.

to exude joy
in the midst of a challenge.

to make your optimism known
to the non believers.

to reach out
to those you love
and not wait for them to make the first
move.

to create the feeling of self love...
just because.

to feel gritty and pretty
as you journey through life
with your inner compass guiding your way.

04

as the tree inspires

trees are living embodiments
of rising up,
growing toward the light
and taking up space
above and below the surface.

the root system of a tree
is absolutely incredible.
its ability to bend and twist around
other neighboring trees' roots
while maintaining its own life force
is inspiring.
this magical and perfect chaos
underground
allows a tree to soar.

when i'm working on cultivating better
boundaries,
i will look at a tree
and learn from it.
it cannot shrink its footprint
to accommodate another tree.
it never hides its essence
or tries to morph into

another type of tree.
it thrives as itself.
it takes up space.
it opens up to the sun.
it has nothing to hide.

05

to say no

how do you say no
when you've always said yes?
it only takes a moment,
but it may prevent
a lifetime of discomfort.

write a script,
practice it,
believe that you can do it.
understand that you will feel discomfort.
you've put everyone else first,
now it's time to put you first.
accept this.
take that first step.

you cannot save anyone else but yourself.
they will get over your no.
they will move on.
you will move on.

see your first chances
to say no
as opportunities to grow
and develop a new muscle.

it will get easier.
you will allow your life
to open up to
bigger and bolder opportunities.
you will see yourself in a better light.
you will feel like your own hero.
after all,
isn't that the ultimate goal?

06

raindrops

little sprinkles of water
that bounce on my skin,
you remind me to be present in this moment.
your birth from the sky
happens quickly and swiftly.
you ignite an immediate response
in those who feel your presence.

the splash of your essence
sparks nostalgic joy in those
of us who allow it.
you radiate a message from the sky
in your simplicity.
there is no escaping your web of interaction,
for you are all encompassing.

your playful presence
magically turns the mundane
into something memorable.

thank you for bringing me
into the present moment.

07

i am the woman that i create

when i take responsibility
for my life,
i feel powerful.
i become the hero of my story.
this brings the flow of life
to me
and sets the framework
for proper action and work.

i am creating the woman
that i want to be.
i am becoming my own hero.
this thesis drives
every decision that i make.
it evokes rational optimism,
confidence
and strength;
because at all times
i know my intention.

08

what i want

rather than circle around
what i truly want,
i now proudly and easily convey
this message.
in every situation,
i allow myself to catch up
to my higher self
and get to the truth.

if i am not sure what it is that i want,
i give myself time and space
to discover what that is.

once i know what i want,
i can focus my energy
on that outcome.
energy needs direction.
goals need focus.
in order to determine my goals,
i must know what i want in life.

09

i choose my best self

in order to love all of you,
i must love all of me.
this love
is reached when i
exude my best self.
when i do not meet personal expectations,
my heart hurts.
i weep inside
and take it out on you.
my pain is transferred onto you.
then, my original pain increases
and this cycle ensues.

i choose my best self.
i choose to do
what i need to do to be this version.
by doing so,
i will open my heart fully
to me,
to you.

10

opening up to joy

the call to joy
was initiated in the moment
that we arrived on the planet.
our ability to see the signs of joy
and experience its essence
can lessen with time.

other humans may project their
pain and sorrow and fear
onto us,
so our spirit becomes weighed down.
our soul then tries to break through
and speak to us
through signs and messages.

one is aware of this attempt,
but the ability to communicate with our
higher self
can be challenging.
the language of the soul
can go undetected at first.
as a result,
the soul works through the body.

as we learn to open up to joy,
we can learn to understand the language
of our soul.
joy is being present
in your life
at all times.
joy is not labeling experiences as
good or bad
and showing up for everything fully.

11

to observe rather than
to identify with

when we feel something,
we tend to identify with it
and make it part of who we are.

the intensity of the emotion
seems to blind its recipient
into thinking it is now an adjective
in which to describe them.

what if we label intense feelings
as passing thoughts
and not cling to their meaning and origin?

these experiences are not identifiers,
rather they are something we feel and
move on from.
as humans, we tend to give labels to things
and then latch onto them for identity.

feel a feeling.
feel it with your entire being.
identify it and move on.

live your life
creating energy
rather than reacting to
the energy of feelings.

12

you are who you create

who do you desire to be?
become her
by your actions,
state of mind,
and inner dialogue.
the external world will
follow your lead.

you are who you create.
she lies dormant inside of you
until you summon her essence.

her achievements will exude
from your being
once you believe.
your faith in yourself
will soar to new heights
as you carry yourself in this new way.

you are who you create.
create with purpose and intention
and become your own hero.

13

take up space

enter the room as the
woman you want to be.
show others who you are
by how you treat yourself.

you are the star of your show.
fill the room with your presence.

you no longer hide within
the excuses from your past.
those attempts to hide your power
were part of your process
to get where you're at now.

take up space with your voice.
take up space with your heart.
take up space with your energy.
the room is yours to fill.

van ekeren

chapter six

the sun's passion

01

the sun's passion

let your passion run as intense
as the heat of the sun.
let this fuel burn inside of you
and show you how to
apply focus to your gifts.

let your passion be crafted
with skill
and never run too wildly.
the brightest fruits
blossom from nurtured trees.

let your heart sing openly and love freely.
allow your insides to be changed
by your past story
and excited for your future story.

let your ambition grow alongside your vision
allowing all joyful possibilities
a proper chance.
breathe in the sun's rays
and know that your energy pulsates from your
being with such ferventness.

02

go out and get it

get up
and jump into the discomfort.
there is no other way.
take ease in knowing
that all heroes face
this tension.
those that are remembered
did not stop
when they were challenged.

you have it in you
to discover who you are
and become her.
you are the hero of your story.
go out and and act like it.
jump into your journey
and steer.

03

the calm after the storm

after mother earth
unleashes her storm of tears
on those of who inhabit
her space,
the calm surfaces.
the chaos of a storm
gives us a metaphor
for our own inner turmoil.
the pain,
the worries,
the anxiety
that can surface within
feel so intense
and smothering.
just as the storm clouds
encapsulate every patch of sky,
our thoughts can consume us
in the midst of an emotional attack.
that moment may feel like an eternity.
but just know,
it will pass.
every storm passes
and every inner turmoil will eventually pass.
do not succumb to it.

breathe.

look up.

ask for help.

mother earth shows us

that all living organisms must

cycle through

various stages.

allow your coping muscle

to grow and expand.

your ability to cope

with the thoughts will improve.

there is always

the calm after the storm.

there is always a relief

from the strife.

04

light

when light hits an object,
a shadow is made.
our eyes are not scared of
the shadows we see
in the external world.

why are we so frightened
of the shadows inside of us?

darkness always accompanies the light.

when you interact with a soul
with a tremendous light,
know they carry a tremendous darkness.
this is life as a human.
it is how one interacts
with their dark side that matters.

this personal approach
is learned,
is mirrored,
is instinctual.
it is the most important part of your psyche.
yes, it can be broken down

into smaller observatory traits
like habits or addictions or personality,
but it is part of a bigger approach
that one embodies.

how do you handle the darkness
within and around?

observe yourself.
accept where you're at.
set the intention to operate at
your fullest light
and watch the lessons ensue.
when you have your intention
at the forefront
of your brain,
you will always succeed.

van ekeren

05

to create confidence

you do not have to wait
for confidence to show up
to act.
confidence will never just appear,
it is created from within.

you have to show up,
face your fear
and then allow
the flow of life
to transmute this energy.
fear is your fuel.
it will be alchemized into confidence
when you take that leap.

you have the ability
to create confidence
when you act.
it takes one decision
and one million future decisions
to continue on your path.
choose your lane
and keep on driving.

06

that secret inside

that inner light,

that inner drive,

that secret that lies inside

each one of us

is the one thing that

we are taught to hide.

the notion of equality

that one strives to promote

may be internally misunderstood.

equality means

all beings are equally equipped

to express their inner light.

everyone has a different glow

and sparkle to their light.

when you sense that one does not

have your intensity,

your speciality,

your talents,

your character,

your self will,

do not back down or dim yours.

equality will shine through

when we all deeply connect

to our genius.

07

that first date with life

keeping the spark alive
in your life
takes work and dedication.
as humans
we project our worries onto others
to justify our decisions.
we rationalize our
addiction to fear
encouraging others
to do the same.
this cycle continues
until one has the eyes to see
their contribution within it.
step out of this pattern
and shine your brilliant light.

treat everyday
like you're on
a first date with life.

being on a first date
brings forward an unparalleled effort
that one usually doesn't tap into.
why not?

it is work
and can feel uncomfortable,
and we continually seek comfort.
the art of not putting ourselves out there
has become a decadent indulgence.

let your guard down
and show up on that
first date with your life.
put on your favorite outfit
and strut your stuff.
don't wait until
next time,
jump into being your best self
today.
lean into the discomfort
and be proud that you're
putting yourself out there.
show people who you are.

08

let others do their work

i want to help you
in order to show you that i love you.
i want to do your work for you
so you do not have to feel discomfort.
this is actually a selfish act
on my part.
unknowingly, i am taking away
your life experiences
that will help you grow.
my passion to share love
can hinder boundaries and
mask proper intention
when i so willingly jump in
and try to fix things for you.

i choose to let you do your work.
i will not be so ready and willing
to provide for you
what you need.
this will hurt at first,
but it will be the best
for both of us.
i trust that we can support one another
in a new and healthy way.

09

it's time for you to shine

you have been holding yourself back
for so long now.
you thought something bad would happen
if you showed life that you were
open and willing.

showing life that you are ready
to experience its essence opens the door
that you have been working on opening.
your previous attempts
were not made in vain
because they got you here.

it is time for you to shine now.
life will not ask anything of you
that you are not ready for.
the juicy layers of experience
are oozing with possibilities.

you are ready for this next chapter.
life beckons.
answer it.

van ekeren

chapter seven

exploring the terrain

01

exploring the terrain

i try to wrap my brain
around the magic
and the music
of this life as a human.
sometimes the melody of life
is loud and thunderous
and at other times,
it's lightly playing in the background
like a piano player at a small bar.

when my eyes are clear,
i can see the magic all around me.
i feel my heart beat with
rhythmic joy
and my blood flow with gumption.
when my mind is open
to possibilities,
i see other humans as friends
and teachers
always willing to lend a hand.

tending to the soil of my mind
is a task that i regard highly.
i try to define my ways

and stick to a plan,
yet this project requires full devotion
and defies all maps.
what works today
may not work tomorrow.
this is how my mind
keeps me thinking
in new ways.
the freshness of a new tactic
to massage and enhance
my brain muscle
is exciting.

the music inside of us
will never cease
regardless of what the critics say.
relying on my intuitive muscles
requires continuous care and consistency.
i get to learn more
about myself everyday.
i get to do the inner work
and strengthen my voice.
i get to sing the song within
adapting to what's around me.

02

the rose

to watch how beauty dances,
one must look to a rose.
it dazzles our senses with its
form, shape, scent and touch.
it reaches its prime
and then allows itself to gracefully
fade away from existence.
it embraces our attention
and flourishes in the limelight.
it willingly puts up boundaries
through the sense of touch
hurting anyone who gets too
close in a certain way.
the gift that a rose gives
the air
cannot be described,
it must be experienced.

the rose
doesn't apologize for its
beauty
nor its thorns.
the rose
knows of its power,

yet basks in its vulnerability.

the rose embodies its role

on this planet

never withdrawing its playfulness.

the rose bends

and dances with humanity

achieving its purpose

in this simple act.

03

the laughter in nature

why are you so serious?
you are a product of nature
and she is full of joy and laughter.
when in the midst of pain,
remember how you are a part of something
so much bigger than you
that laughs and smiles through creation.

when we get out of alignment
and think we are alone,
or the only one going through something,
we ache so deeply.
nature calls to us during this time.
she reminds us
that we are all in this together.
the trees have no insurance that
the sky will feed them with its sun and water.
they trust anyway.

as a human,
we have no insurance
that tomorrow will be okay.
yet, we continue living.
nature is not perfect

and has never asked us to be.
what are our needs and wants?
and why?

nature exudes gratitude.

when we can disconnect
from our created worries and fears,
we can connect to this vibration
of joy
and laughter
and pure acceptance.
there is no better time
to be alive
than right now.

04

new days bring new thoughts

the mental.
the physical.
what proceeds the other?
the life lived inside of our heads
fascinates me.

we get to work on
the soil of our brain,
the landscape of our thoughts.
we have the honor
to pull out the weeds
and plant new thoughts.

when we allow the darker ones
to bubble up and not run from them,
they do not have control over us.
thoughts are just visitors
to our mind muscle.
they do not belong to you
just as the sounds you hear
do not belong to you.
it's okay that you have dark thoughts.
it's okay that you strive to have joyful
thoughts.

everything passes.
ride every wave that
life presents
to you
and feel the nourishment
this provides.

05

levels of understanding

i understand to the best of my ability
today,
at this moment.
i am open to the next level of understanding
and the next
and the next.
this ladder awaits my grasp
and focus
and study.
i ask my invisible guides for help continuously
as i climb.
sometimes i have no idea where
my foot will land,
but i persist.
this trust continues
to grow and cultivate within.
i know that i am being lead.
i trust.

06

when you like being around yourself

a change occurs in one's life
when they truly enjoy
being in their own company.

there's a freedom
that emerges from within
that's always been there.

the need to be a certain person
or be seen in a particular way
fades away completely.

stresses reveal themselves
and you suddenly have the foresight
to not be swayed by these triggers.

the art that's inside you
begins to sing
and show itself in all sorts of mediums.

you feel happy
and know that's enough.

07

the way

the only way
is your way.
life has a sense of humor
and asks
that you get out of your way
to find your way.
you must surrender
and accept
that the invisible forces
around you
know more.

i know you know this,
but it is so hard to trust
in what we cannot see.
we need answers.
we need facts.
we need to see evidence of
the existence of the unseen realms.

the invisible forces
that surround us
act as our anchor into the present moment.

they are always working
in our favor
helping us enjoy this experience called life.

the smell of fresh air,
the rising of the sun,
the glow of the moon
act as guide posts
to heed their messages.
one needs to be present
to be able to absorb
the many layers of life.

when we ask to see
then we are led to see.
ask now
and watch for your answers.

08

to take responsibility

i used to blame you
for my pain
for my discomfort
for my lack of abilities.
i see now
how
this kept
feeding my insecurities.

any lack within
i blamed another for.
any situation that
i wasn't proud of
must've been their fault
not mine.
any moment i acted
without grace
was a time to point the finger
at someone else.

i acknowledge this habit,
which allows me
to heal from it.
i take responsibility

for my life
and honor my past.
this shift
creates space
for my future to blossom.

it was never your fault,
it was my inability to see me.
i choose to take responsibility
with my eyes fully open to see
my courage
my strength
my willingness to work
and my desire to grow.

09

the poet's dream

when you read my words
and tell me that they
changed you,
i am living my dream.
i get to create a relationship
with you
through words on a page.
i honor this.

i write to connect the dots
of this life.
i write to discover how to
get through emotional discomfort.
i write to create and craft
a life worth living.

words connect us all
on this journey.
nothing is so bad as it seems
when you can get it
out of your head
and into the air.
words are the way we do this.

being a poet
doesn't mean i know it all.
i just enjoy
the art of connecting the dots
through language.

van ekeren

10

the wonder of living

those before us
have done it.
those amongst us
are doing it.
i am speaking of those
who are able to see
the wonder
of this experience of life
rather than judge the outcome.

they have developed the eyes to see,
the ears to hear,
and the heart to love unconditionally.
they can see possibilities
where most cannot.
they can intuitively reconnect to our source
when triggered by the ways of the world.

they've done the inner work
that allows them
to do their earthly work.

they've accepted reality as it is now
and live in today

as their best self.
they lovingly utilize self discipline
in every situation
knowing that this brings far more joy
than anything else.

their hearts are full
and their minds are joyous.
they're ready to
discover the wonder that lies
in front of them.

11

sunny days

the sunny days
already live
within me.
they always have.

the joy that accompanies
such days
is my continual partner.

we work together
to see life
through our sunny colored lens.

it's simple really,
we get to make
the choice
to exist in our created mindset.

just as sunny days
radiate warmth,
so does this lifestyle.

one is never alone
when they've chosen
this lifelong perspective.

let's share our excitement
and never shy away
from sharing our approach to life
with others.

our sunny days will
continue to shine
and light our way.

About the Author

Nikki Van Ekeren encourages one to become their most authentic self through the power of words. She enjoys the art of connecting through language.

Nikki is a west coast gal living in Brooklyn. When she is not writing or reading, you can find her painting in her studio or taking a walk in nature.

van ekeren